The Tibetan Book of the Dead
for Reading Aloud

The Tibetan Book of the Dead for Reading Aloud

adapted by
Jean-Claude van Itallie

photos of *Tibetan Book of the Dead* performance at La MaMa E.T.C. by
Gerry Vezzuso

other illustrations selected by
Deborah E. Klimburg-Salter
Professor of Oriental Art, University of Vienna

Introduction by
Judith L. Lief
Former Dean of Naropa Institute, Boulder, Colorado

North Atlantic Books
Berkeley, California

The Tibetan Book of the Dead for Reading Aloud

The Tibetan Book of the Dead for Reading Aloud has been edited by the author for this edition. The acting version of van Itallie's play, *The Tibetan Book of the Dead*, including stage directions, is available from Dramatists Play Service, 440 Park Avenue South, NY, NY 10016, who control stock and amateur performance rights.

Published by
North Atlantic Books
P.O. Box 12327
Berkeley, California 94712

Cover photograph of *Tibetan Book of the Dead* performance at La MaMa E.T.C.
© Gerry Vezzuso

Author photo © 1995 by Susan Johann

Cover and book design by Paula Morrison

Printed in Singapore

The Tibetan Book of the Dead for Reading Aloud is sponsored by the Society for the Study of Native Arts and Sciences, a nonprofit educational corporation whose goals are to develop an educational and crosscultural perspective linking various scientific, social, and artistic fields; to nurture a holistic view of arts, sciences, humanities, and healing; and to publish and distribute literature on the relationship of mind, body, and nature.

Library of Congress Cataloging-in-Publication Data
  Jean-Claude van Itallie
    The Tibetan book of the dead for reading aloud / Jean-Claude van Itallie.
      p. cm.
    ISBN 1-55643-273-9 (pbk.)
    1. Intermediate state—Buddhism—Early works to 1800. 2. Death—Religious aspects—Buddhism—Early works to 1800. 3. Funeral rites and ceremonies, Buddhist—Early works to 1800. I. van Itallie, Jean-Claude, 1936–   . II. Title.
  BQ4490.K3713 1998
  194.3'423—dc21
                                   97-49579
                                       CIP

2 3 4 5 6 7 8 9 TWP 07 06 05 04 03

for my teachers
Chögyam Trungpa, Rinpoche,
and
Ellen Stewart
with love and respect

Pious tradition considers the Bardo Thodol to be a "Hidden Treasure" (Terma), first revealed by Pädmasambhava in the 8th century and redis-covered by one of the eight great treasure seekers (Terton), the Rig din Karma Ling pa. The text survives in a number of written forms; the most ancient, a simplified version, was found in Tun hung. Oral commentary has been a critical component of the transmission of this sacred text for 1200 years. In that sense, van Itallie's adaptation, based on the English translation and oral teachings of the great Karma Kagyu teacher Chögyam Trungpa, Rinpoche, is part of the long and authentic history of this teaching.

Jean-Claude van Itallie first adapted this ancient Tibetan text as a play, *The Tibetan Book of the Dead, or How Not To Do It Again,* which pre-miered at La MaMa Experimental Theatre Club in New York City, January 14, 1983, directed by Assurbanipal Babilla; produced by Ellen Stewart; set by Jun Maeda; music by Steve Gorn; production photographed by Gerry Vezzuso; floor mandala painted by Louise Baum; performers: Cristo-bal Carambo, Du-Yee Chang, Sussan Deihim, Kevin O'Meara, Hooshang Touzie, Ching Valdez, and Robinson Youngblood.

The script of van Itallie's play became the libretto for an opera with music composed by Ricky Ian Gordon: *The Tibetan Book of the Dead, or The Great Liberation Through Hearing,* which premiered at both the Hous-ton Grand Opera Studio and the American Musical Theater Festival in Philadelphia in June, 1996.

The author would like to thank his many friends who helped to make this book possible, especially Lillian Butler, Rand Engel, Edith Goldenhar, and Deborah E. Klimburg-Salter for their invaluable editorial accompaniment.

Introduction

The Tibetan Book of the Dead is a manual traditionally read aloud to the dying and the dead by a spiritual teacher or a friend. It is a teaching expressed through the spoken word.

One of the earliest teachers to bring Buddhism to Tibet, Pädmasambhava, popularly called Precious Guru (*Guru Rinpoche*), is said to have composed *The Tibetan Book of the Dead* around the eighth century A.D. It was rediscovered in Tibet as a Hidden Treasure (*Terton*) around six hundred years ago and is part of the everyday culture of Tibetan Buddhism.

The Tibetan Book of the Dead contains practical navigational instructions of urgent use on the journey that starts with dying and continues in the days following death. A guide-book to the "in-between place," it instructs how to avoid the suffering caused by the confusion of constantly discursive thoughts.

The Tibetan Book of the Dead is also for the living, a meditation manual on how to pay attention despite the distraction of our daily worlds.

The Tibetan Book of the Dead for Reading Aloud is offered here in a form in which *The Tibetan Book of the Dead* can easily be read to oneself or to a friend at a time of need. A playwright and a practicing Tibetan Buddhist for thirty years, I wrote it because I felt a need to make the *Tibetan Book of the Dead* as readily available as a book of poems.

In *The Tibetan Book of the Dead,* the traveler-after-death starts "at the top" with an experience of the clear white light of universal mind. This light, most visible at the moment of death, is our best opportunity. If we recognize it as our own fully-awakened nature, we may merge with it.

If not, however, the five peaceful manifestations of universal energy each appear in turn. (Presumably these energies appear differently to each person.) Pay attention, says *The Tibetan Book of the Dead:* These peaceful energies are you too.

But if we don't recognize these as emanations of our own mind, then the five universal energies will appear again, this time in angry form.

If, despite warnings from the *Book,* we are blinded by fear, and do not recognize the angry energies as emanations of our own mind, we descend further yet. We attempt to return to our former body. We want our possessions back. The voice of a friend reading aloud the *Book* reminds us that we can't return to the past, we must be fearless, we must take this opportunity not to be reborn into a world of tears.

But if we allow ourselves to be pushed even further downward by demons, by old habits of thinking, then we must seek refuge in a womb. "Don't grab just any womb" says the *Book*. The *Book* gives the dead one instructions on how to consciously choose an auspicious place of rebirth.

The Tibetan Book of the Dead reminds us, in living as in dying, to stay alert, to be fearless and undistracted.

The Tibetan Book of the Dead addresses us as "Nobly Born" and "You of Glorious Origin," reminding us that we are ourselves manifestations of universal energy.

Jean-Claude van Itallie
Shantigar Foundation
Rowe, Massachusetts
January, 1998

Foreword

by Judith L. Lief

former Dean of Naropa Institute, Boulder, Colorado

It is my great pleasure to introduce Jean-Claude van Itallie's rendition of this classic text. I believe that *The Tibetan Book of the Dead for Reading Aloud* will benefit countless beings and help make the profound teachings of vajrayana Buddhism more widely known. As each and every one of us will face death sooner or later, and as we all would like to live more sanely and freely, these teachings continue to be relevant in this day and age.

When Trungpa, Rinpoche, was asked whether he would recommend reading *The Tibetan Book of the Dead* to people who were dying, he said it would be far better to present the teachings of the book in one's own words. Instead of reciting a text that would most likely seem unfamiliar and alien, one should speak directly from one's own experience and understanding. That is precisely what Jean-Claude has done.

The Tibetan Book of the Dead for Reading Aloud, originally written as a play, is a freer more poetic rendering of the original Tibetan text. Jean-Claude has removed the many technical terms, and difficult Sanskrit multisyllabics that can be confusing obstacles for western readers. But he has in no way watered down the essential teaching. The themes of the book come through simply and directly, without distortion. Of all the versions available in English, Jean-Claude's version lends itself most readily to reading aloud.

Since *The Tibetan Book of the Dead* was first translated into English by Evans-Wentz in 1927, it has held a fascination for Westerners. Evans-Wentz's translation was one of the first teachings of Tibetan Buddhism to reach an English-speaking audience. Soon after, *The Tibetan Book of the Dead* was translated into several other Western languages. Carl Jung was so struck by this work that he composed a psychological commentary for the Swiss edition, published in 1938. Dr. Jung's commentary was later translated into English, and included with subsequent English editions of the text.

Contact of Westerners with Tibetan teachers was very limited until the 1970s, when a number of Tibetans, who had been forced to flee Tibet, took up residence in the West and began to work with Western students. This was a significant development, for previously only those Westerners both daring enough to travel to Tibet and willing to learn Tibetan had access to this tradition.

One of the first teachers to come to the West was Venerable Chögyam Trungpa, Rinpoche, the eleventh Trungpa Tulku, who settled in North America after residing briefly in England and Scotland. It happened that his monastery, Surmang, specialized in the teachings of *The Great Liberation through Hearing in the Bardo,* the text translated by Evans-Wentz as *The Tibetan Book of the Dead.*

While teaching on this topic in Vermont, Trungpa, Rinpoche, noticed that his students had difficulties with the outdated tone and language of the Evans-Wentz version. The direct and earthy quality of the original text had been lost, and an element of religiosity had crept in. Therefore, Trungpa, Rinpoche, working with Francesca Freemantle, published a new translation in 1975. Trungpa, Rinpoche, wanted to use simple straightforward English in his translation so that the teachings could come through clearly and without pretense.

A third translation was done in 1966 by Professor Robert Thurman. His translation was also based on the attempt to make this text accessible to Westerners and includes translations of related texts that were previously unavailable, as well as a detailed commentary by Thurman.

The teachings on *bardo,* or the intermediate state, that are the basis of this book come out of the rich tradition of vajrayana Buddhism. The vajrayana tradition is characterized by astute psychological observation and rigorous meditation practice. Although it has many complexities, fundamentally it is based on two simple and practical foundations: mindfulness-awareness practice and the cultivation of loving-kindness.

According to bardo teachings, just as now we are journeying from birth toward death, after death there is a parallel journey that covers the period from the moment of death to our subsequent rebirth. There is a continuous succession of intermediate states as we cycle from birth to death to birth to death. Even within our lifetime, we experience birth and death daily in the form of the ever-changing and unpredictable nature of our life in the world.

The fact of change is a powerful teaching and a call to wake up. It is an opportunity to drop illusions and face reality. Yet it is not easy to drop habits we have carefully built up over time, habits of struggle and mistaken identity, habits based on fear and hesitation to think big. According to *The Tibetan Book of the Dead,* if you courageously look into the roots of your own confusion, you will undermine it, since only if you look away can it continue to thrive. In the process, you will come face to face with your own innate wisdom, in the form of radiant visions of peaceful and wrathful deities. However, although the teachings are presented in the form of colorful images and deities, what you are dealing with is none other than your own state of mind, its wisdom as well as its confusion.

The Tibetan Book of the Dead has three parts. The first has to do with the shock at the moment of death. The second has to do with the illusory and dreamlike journey of severing your ties with this life. The third has to do with the fear of groundlessness and the urge to take solid form in a new existence. In each of these three sections you face choices. There are countless opportunities for awakening as you go through the bardo, but it is up to you whether you succumb to hesitation and the lure of the familiar or extend yourself and take a leap.

Given the intensity of the bardo experience, it makes sense to prepare yourself in some way. Reading and studying a text such as *The Tibetan of the Dead* is a powerful start. It is meant to be read and reread. But conceptual knowledge alone is limited. In order to deepen your understanding of these teachings, you need to apply them personally. You need to look into your *own* life: your own relationship to change and death, your own pattern of confusion and your own spiritual practice.

The Tibetan Book of the Dead is not a gimmick, a formula to get you through the process of death. It comes back again and again to very basic instructions: do not let your mind wander; pay attention; cultivate compassion; be stable; if you have received a spiritual practice do not wait, do it now; if you have a teacher, seek out his help. You are constantly thrown back on yourself and — as Trungpa, Rinpoche, repeatedly said — the realization that, "It is up to you, Sweetheart!"

The Tibetan Book of the Dead
for Reading Aloud

To Friends of the Dying

Oh you,
Who have come to this place,
Sisters and brothers, friends,
This person is dying.
She (he) has not chosen to do so.
She is suffering greatly.
She has no home, no friends.
Falling as from a cliff,
She is entering a strange forest.

Driven by the winds, swept by the ocean,
She feels no solid ground.
She is embarking on a great battle.
Moved from state to state,
She is alone and helpless.
Embrace her with your love.

The Dying

My friend,
You are feeling heavy,
You can no longer open or close your eyes.
Blue, yellow, red and green are turning white.
Logic and the chair and the table are dissolving.
The earth element in your body is dissolving into water.

My friend,
Your mind is losing its hold,
You grab at this,
You grab at that.
Your blood is slowing,
You feel faint.
Logic and the chair and the table are dissolving.
No more external sounds,
No more internal sounds.
You have no saliva, no sweat.
Everything is drying.
The water element in your body is dissolving into fire.

My friend,
Now you feel cold.
You have a sense of far-off vastness,
And you seem to see fireflies, or sparks
Within smoke.
You can't get enough air.
You are losing ground.
Everything seems hollow.
You try to remember who you love.
The fire element in your body is dissolving into air.

My friend,
Now you are losing your last touch with the world:
Your sense of taste.
The last sign:
A sputtering butter lamp,
About to go out.
The air element in your body is dissolving into ether.

The Moment of Death

My friend,
Now is the moment of death.

The time has come for you to start out.
You are going home.

Oh, Nobly Born,
Now is the moment.
Before you is mind, open and wide as space,
Simple, without center or circumference.

Now is the moment of death.
Your mind in this moment is total transparency:
No color, no substance, empty,
Sparkling, pure and vibrant,
A mass of light
Not stopped by any obstacle.
It has neither beginning nor end.
Go toward the light.
Merge with it.
Merge with the light.

Death has happened.
It happens to everyone.

Clear White Light

Merge with the clear white light.
Don't long for what's finished.
You can't stay here anymore.
Death has happened.
It happens to everyone.
In this crucial moment,
Don't be afraid.
Whatever appears,
Recognize as the form of your own thoughts.

Please don't be afraid of your own radiance.
You no longer have a physical body.
Death has happened.
So nothing can hurt you.
You can't die again.
Don't be afraid.
Merge with the light. Merge. Merge.

The Peaceful Energies

As you have not merged with the clear white light,
The five families, the universal energies,
Will now appear
In peaceful aspect, each in turn:

In the center
You find a place to make camp,
A place where others have been before you,
A muddy field between winter and spring.
Here the clear white sky of All-Embracing Wisdom spreads.
The great emperor with his consort
Arises in the center of your being.
Oh, Noble One, do not separate yourself from him.
Oh, Noble One, do not be frightened.
Abandon all fixed points of view.
Be like an ocean with no boat.
Be like an ocean with no boat,
All directions at once.

But if you hide in a world of bliss
You won't be able to think.
Don't pull back.
Be like an ocean with no boat,
Oh, Nobly Born.

So remain awake, oh Nobly Born.
Merge with All-Encompassing Wisdom
At the center of your being.
Merge. Merge. Merge.

Now in the east
The blue water element sparkles:
The Diamond One and his consort
Shine from the Realm of Complete Joy,
Unshakeable Mirror-like Wisdom,
Lake with no ripples
Reflecting the world as it is,
Intelligence piercing your heart like an icicle.
Don't be angry, Oh Noble One.
Water will purify.
This is the sharp sword of vision,
Lightning insight,
Blue-white of winter,
Clarity of sunrise,
Diamond Mind.

But if you are angry,
If you flee
To the smoky worlds of hate,
You'll feel such pain
You won't be able to think.

So remain alert, Oh Nobly Born.
The diamond rays are your own diamond rays.
Recognize them.
Merge. Merge. Merge.

Now from the south
The earth element shines yellow like gold.
From the Realm of the Great and the Glorious
Comes the Splendid King and his court
All bejeweled:
The abundance of harvest,
Generosity and wealth,
Kingly Wisdom of Equanimity,
The sun.

But if you are proud
And hide in the human world,
You experience once again
Birth, suffering, old age and death.

So, Nobly Born,
Rest in the golden rays.
Merge. Merge. Merge.

Now from the west
The fire element glows everywhere red:
The sunset.
From the Realm of Ecstasy
Glows the Compassionate One on his peacock throne.
Oh, Nobly Born,
This is the warmth of your own heart.
Embrace it.
This is springtime, blossoms,
Fawns dancing in a field,
Beauty touching your heart,
Discriminating Wisdom.

But if you inflame love into desire,
You will become a hungry ghost,
Always hungry, always thirsty.

So, Nobly Born,
Rest, rest
In the rosy light of Compassion.
Merge.

Now from the green north
Arises the air element, the wind,
Stirring your heart.
From the Realm of the Accomplishment of All Actions
Comes the Great Doer,
On the back of his powerful bird,
The wings of the bird raising the wind,
Stirring the leaves,
Swaying the birches,
Rippling the green grasses of summer,
Filling your ears with sound.
Be one with this activity.

But if out of envy
You hide in the world of the jealous,
You'll never stop striving, reaching, competing,
Striving, reaching, competing.

So join the shining wind itself.
This the way of your own mind.
Be the wind.
Be the wind.

The Rainbow Dance

The peaceful energies
Appear together now, dancing.
Merge with the rainbow.

The Dreamlike Realms

Oh, you of glorious origin,
You saw the families of organic energy.
If you had recognized their radiance
As your own,
You would have dissolved into the rainbow.

But you are still wandering.
Don't be afraid.
The four directions of your own heart
Are old friends,
The play of your own mind.
Piercing doubt,
Free of all thoughts,
Greet them as a mother embraces her child.
They will dissolve into you
And you will attain illumination.

But if you are afraid,
And attracted again to familiar dreamlike realms,
The realms of the gods,
The jealous gods,
The humans,
The animals,
The hungry ghosts,
Or the hell beings,
Then you will be reborn
Into the ocean of miseries.

So remain free of all thoughts.

If you are drawn to the god realm,
To the dreamy world of the blissful,
You will no longer be able to think.

So remain alert,
Oh, Nobly Born,
And watch, watch.

If you are pulled to the jealous god realm,
To the cloudy world of the ambitious,
Oh, Nobly Born,
You will never stop striving, reaching, competing.

So watch, watch.

Oh, Nobly Born,
Even if you hide in the human realm,
Constantly adjusting this and that,
Trying to be comfortable,
You will experience once again
Birth,
Suffering,
Old age, and death.

So watch, watch.

And don't be attracted to the colorless animal realm,
Oh, Nobly Born,
For there are no words there, no humor.

So watch, watch.

Oh, Nobly Born,
If you are addicted to the half-world
Of the hungry ghosts,
You will only desire
And desire.
Never satisfied,
You will develop a large belly and a small throat.

So watch, watch.

And don't be drawn
To the smoky realms of hate,
Or you'll feel such pain
You won't be able to think.
So remain alert, oh Nobly Born.
Watch, watch.

Don't be reborn
Into the ocean of miseries.
Remain free of all thoughts.
Oh, You of Glorious Origin,
Watch, watch.
Don't be distracted.
Don't escape the rainbow dance of your own mind.
Iti samaya rigya rigya rigya.

The Angry Energies

The five families of universal energies
Will now appear to you
In wrathful aspect,
Each thundering in turn.
Don't be terrified.

The huge stone-like white demon
Mired in the center of your mind
Is your own ignorance.
Recognize it, oh Nobly Born.

The furious ice blue demon
Freezing the east of your mind
Is your own hatred.
Recognize it, oh Nobly Born.

The stubborn yellow tyrant
Enthroned in the south of your mind
Is your own pride.
Recognize it, oh Nobly Born.

The voracious red mouth
Devouring the west of your mind
Is your own lust.
Recognize it, oh Nobly Born.

The hideous green monster
Twisting the north of your mind
Is your own envy.
Recognize it, oh Nobly Born.

Mahakala

Many-armed Mahakala,
Fierce and dark protector of wisdom,
Now appears,
Terrifying and powerful.

Recognize your darker self.

The Lord of Death

Now the Lord of Death appears:
"This old man, he plays one.
  He plays knick-knack on my thumb,
  With a knick-knack, paddy whack,
  Give the dog a bone.
  This old man goes rolling home."

Oh, You of Glorious Origin, don't be afraid.
Even if you were cut into little pieces,
You couldn't possibly die again.
Emptiness cannot harm emptiness.

The Wanderer's Prayer

As I wander through worlds of illusion,
May I remain confident
And remember my own mind.
May the Five Wisdoms shine.
May I recognize myself.

When earth, water, fire, air or ether rise up against me,
May I remember my teachers.
May blessings go before me,
And compassionate Queens of Space
Help me to cross this dangerous place.

When my old ways of thinking
Cause me to wander,
May I hear blessings
Even in the roar of a thousand thunders
And recognize this realm of shadows
For what it is.

Confident, may I see the Universal Energies.
Sarva Mangalam.

Realizing I Am Dead

I saw peaceful and angry energies
But I didn't recognize them as my own,
So I fainted.

When I was alive,
I was blind, I limped, and I was mute.
But now my eyes distinguish.
My ears hear.
I can move easily.
My voice is clear.
So I know I must be dead.
If I can remember that,
I won't be lost.
I won't need to be reborn.

I no longer have a physical body.
I am wandering.
I have amazing powers.
I can go where I wish in the time it takes to open
Or close my hand.

I see my house and my friends
As if in a dream.
I call out: Hello. I'm here.
No answer.
What am I to do?
I'm like a fish on hot sand.
My mind wanders like a lost feather.
I'm here. Don't cry. I'm here.
No answer.
So.
I am dead.

Pursued By Demons

Oh, Nobly Born, the demons that pursue you now:
The mountains crumbling,
The earthquakes,
The tidal waves and fires,
The approaching armies,
The hunters and the wild beasts,
All these spring from your own mind.

Passion, Aggression and Ignorance:
Three cliffs.
You are about to fall.
Oh, Nobly Born, recognize the state of becoming.

You see your home and your friends
But they cannot see you,
So you must be dead.

You ask: where is my body?
Winter has frozen your corpse,
Or summer decomposed it.
Where is my body?
Your friends have burned it,
Or fed it to the birds.
Where is my body?
You feel squeezed between rocks
And tossed by the winds.
I want my body.

You feel on trial.
Your judges speak:
One good deed. One bad deed.
One good deed. One bad deed.
One good deed. One bad deed.
One bad deed.   One bad deed.
No, it's not true, you say, not that many.

Oh, Nobly Born, you can't die now.
You have no body. You're already dead.
The demons are your own imagining.
Truly, you are empty.
Oh, Nobly Born,
Emptiness is terrifying, it's true,
But emptiness is light,
And light is only mind,
So don't be afraid.

Oh, You of Glorious Origin, watch out.
If you allow yourself to be distracted,
You will fall into a trap.
From moment to moment
You hurt, you want.
Back, forth, hurt, want, hurt, want.

The ritual for the dead is carried out for you.
Its performance is less than perfect.
Don't attach yourself to this imperfection.
Watch out. Mindless anger is a trap.
You worry: do your friends love you?
Watch out. Mindless passion is a trap.
The impurities you see in the ceremony
Are your own face
Reflected in a mirror.

Your spirit is light now.
It moves. It has no anchor.
Every thought radiating from you has power.
Don't pity yourself.
Don't make yourself small.
You want your things
But they are of no use to you now.
Let whoever has them have them.
By wanting and wanting
You become a hungry ghost.

Hungry Ghosts

You come to a hiding place at last.
You think you are happy.
But listen. This is important:
Be careful.
You could be born here
And have to suffer life again.

So far you've not recognized your own light.
Do so now.
Close the entrance to the womb.
Even now there is no need to be reborn.
You have no body to cast a shadow.

Oh, Nobly Born,
If you are pulled to the half-world of the hungry ghosts
You will only want and want and want,
And never be satisfied.

In the lake of your own mind
There is no moon reflected.

Love-Making

Oh, You of Glorious Origin,
Don't be distracted.
Ride the horse of bliss and emptiness
Which is your own mind.
Hold the bridle tight,
And thus close the opening to the womb.

You see couples making love.
Don't be distracted.
Don't get caught between man and woman.
If you were conceived now
You could be born
A horse, a bird, a dog.
If you were born male,
You could be angry at your father,
And want your mother.
If you were born female,
You could be jealous of your mother,
And want your father.
For an instant you would know the bliss
Of sperm meeting egg.
Then you'd develop until
Your body left the womb.
What could be more terrifying?

Father, mother, the great storm:
All are illusion.

Wandering

You've wandered so long
In this muddy swamp.
If you continue to see
What is transparent,
What shimmers, as solid
You will wander further yet.

Your mind itself is only an idea.
It has never been anything more.
You hear only echoes,
You see only dreams.
Cities are mirages.
The mountains are like the moon reflected in water,
Waves of your own mind.
This mind, shimmering, transparent,
Without beginning,
Without obstacle,
Is like water poured into water,
Water poured into water.

Because you are afraid,
You hide in a big house or in a tree,
Or in the cavity of a flower.
Out of fear, to escape your demons,
You are willing to endure anything,
To take whatever body comes.

Oh, You of Glorious Origin,
Best is to rest, empty.

Or, if you can't, join the play of illusion.
Don't attach yourself to this or that.
Becoming illusion's child,
The time has come to choose a body.

Choosing A Home

Your future is beginning to outline itself.
Watch out.
Don't take whatever body appears.
Your future will be colored by
The dreamlike realm that most attracts you:
The realm
Of the gods,
The jealous gods,
The humans,
The animals,
The hungry ghosts,
Or the hell beings.

Watch out.
If you are drawn to cow dung,
Its odor will seem sweet,
And you will be born in a field of dung.
So be careful.
Choose a body to help all living beings.
Be born for the good of all.
Choose now but watch what you choose.
A good home
May be taken for a bad one.
A bad home
May be taken for a good one.

In the east: a lake with geese.
Watch out.
That world may seem full of happiness
But truth does not flourish there.

In the west: a lake with horses.
Watch out.
That world has many joys
But truth does not flourish there.

In the north, life is long and peaceful
By a lake with trees and cows.
But watch out.
Truth does not flourish there.

In the south: a palace.
Enter here like a queen (king),
If you can.

Enter again this theatre of illusion,
This vale of tears.

Walk with your head high.
Call on the forces of compassion.

Entering Again

Enter again
The palace encrusted with gems.
Walk knowingly
In the pleasure gardens:
Bubble of illusion.
Rest in the golden rays.
Sarvamangalam.

About the Illustrations

Page iv: Guru Pädmasambhava, metal alloy, ca. 14th century. Private collection

Pages v, ix, 2, 38, 44, 48, 52, 60: photographs of the performance of *The Tibetan Book of the Dead* at La MaMa E.T.C. © Gerry Vezzuso

Pages xii and 56 (and detail on page 50): Wheel of Existence, Northeastern or Eastern Tibet, 18th or early 19th century, colors on cotton cloth, 109.2 x 86.4 cm. The Newark Museum, Newark, New Jersey, U.S.A. The Newark Museum/Art Source, NY

Page 4, 6, 8, 10, 20, 22, 24, 26: Shantigar movement room wall photographs digitally painted by Paula Morrison

Page 13: ink on paper, Jean-Claude van Itallie

Page 18: Mandala of the Second Stage of the Bardo, 19th century, 87 x 61 cm, watercolor on cotton. Musée Guimet, Paris, France

Page 28: detail, the peaceful dieties from Mandala of Fierce and Tranquil Deities: visions from the Second Stage of the Bardo, Tibet, 18th or 19th century, colors and gold on cotton cloth, 72.4 x 48.3 cm. Photo by John Bigelow Taylor. Collection of The Newark Museum, The Newark Museum, Newark, New Jersey, U.S.A. The Newark Museum/Art Source, NY

Page 34: Chemchoq Heruka and the Five Heruka Buddhas with their Consorts, watercolor on cotton, ca. 18th century. Private collection

Page 36: Mahakala, wall painting, Ta Pho, Protector's Chapel of the Main Temple, 16th century. Photo by Deborah Klimburg-Salter

Page 50: detail of the Realm of the Hungry Ghosts from the Wheel of Existence, Northeastern or Eastern Tibet, 18th or early 19th century, colors on cotton cloth, 109.2 x 86.4 cm. The Newark Museum, Newark, New Jersey, U.S.A. The Newark Museum/Art Source, NY

Page 54: Shantigar. Photo by Gerry Vezzuso

Page 58: Shantigar. Photo by Chögyam Trungpa, Rinpoche

Photo by Susan Johann

Jean-Claude van Itallie, a student of Chögyam Trungpa, Rinpoche, has been a practitioner of Tibetan Buddhism for over thirty years. His play, *The Tibetan Book of the Dead,* premiered at La MaMa E.T.C. in New York City in 1983. Van Itallie has written over thirty plays, musicals, and translations including widely produced versions of Chekhov's four major works. His prize-winning *America Hurrah* is considered the watershed political play of the sixties. He was an early La MaMa playwright and the Playwright-of-the-Ensemble of the Open Theatre for whom he wrote *The Serpent.* Van Itallie's other plays include *King of the United States, Bag Lady, The Traveler,* and *Ancient Boys.* Van Itallie, author of the play writing manual, *The Playwright's Workbook,* has taught play writing and performance in universities and theatres for three decades. As a writer/performer, van Itallie has appeared in *Guys Dreamin'* and in his solo piece, *War, Sex, Singing and Dancing.* He leads workshops in The Healing Power of Theatre around the country. He lives in Western Massachusetts, where he has transformed his farm into Shantigar Foundation: where artistic and spiritual practices meet.